Windows 10

The Ultimate Beginners User Guide

By Bill Vickers

Table of Contents

INTRODUCTION

Windows has finally completed its long anticipated update. Thematically similar and containing much of the more popular Windows 7 platform, the layout will feel familiar and comfortable to users of the older Windows systems whilst providing new and exciting features.

The start menu is back by popular demand and joins a litany of more outstanding improvements, this is widely lauded as being the most feature packed Windows instalment yet. Upgrading to Windows 10 adds new features to the gaming, conference room, desktop, virtual reality, console and mobile environments.

In a bold rebranding Microsoft decided to forego a Windows 9 release and proceeded to 10, having committed substantial resources to making it worthy of a 10/10 rating. The installation process takes somewhere between 20-45 minutes on a typical connection however there are notable departures from previous installations such as the dedicated Welcome Back screen which allows you to sign in and complete setup.

There has been a distinct change in the store presence of Windows 10 which will now be available prepackaged as a USB drive and the traditional DVD disk.

Microsoft have stated downloaded updates will be the norm going forwards This marks a distinct shift towards web updates rather than reselling physical products. Another new development is that Microsoft are now facilitating upgrades from factory preinstalled OEM licenses which is immensely useful and time saving for larger IT networks as going forwards their customary format and reinstall will no longer be necessary as all devices furnished with the OS will now update simultaneously provided that the following system requirements are met:

1. Processor: 1 gigahertz (GHz) or SoC

2. RAM: 1 gigabyte (GB) for 32-bit or 2 GB for 64-bit

3. Hard drive Capacity: 16 GB's for 32-bit OS 20 GB for 64-bit OS

4. Graphics card: DirectX 9 or later with WDDM 1.0 driver

5. Minimum Display: 800x600

The display resolution requirements have been downgraded from 1024x768 to 1024x600. Previously modern applications had a minimum of 1024x768 screen resolution, and reached 1366x768 for the snap feature. If a metro style app were to be launched (e.g. 800x600, 1024x600) the user would simply encounter an error message.

In Windows 10, Modern apps, now rebranded as Universal Windows Apps have identical functionality as all windows apps demonstrating the ability float on the desktop, minimize to the Taskbar; the ever popular Snap feature is now compatible with these universal apps as well.

ARM devices that run Windows RT edition will not receive Windows 10. Microsoft have opted to deliver Windows 10 like features to such devices. Windows and ARM have not parted company with a new class of mobile devices including Microsoft's own Lumia series, 7 inches and smaller continuing to be supported by an ARM based version of Windows 10. The maker community and its famed Raspberry PI device will also have an integrated version of Windows 10.

By building a richer app ecosystem, Microsoft hope to attract new revenue streams such as direct advertising, their own app Store and the encouragement of developer engagement with their platform.

Other developments include the reduced rates OEMs have to pay for licensed Windows 10 content for PCs that are preloaded with the new operating system. All customers however are still expected to purchase licenses as Microsoft have stressed that the update is only free to those who take advantage of it within the first year, after that, anyone who misses out on their introductory offer will have to buy its flagship OS wholesale.

CHAPTER 1
WHAT'S NEW?

Windows 10 has received a broad array of accolades for the innovation and applied research found in their new platform. They have even managed the inevitable problems of the software's infancy extremely well through patching.

Start Menu is back with a twist, a personalisation space where we can customise our layout with select programs, apps, people websites and more. Our account picture now handles all aspects of security with a separate screen.

The Start menu now houses quick links to PC settings, with Document and File Explorer at the top and the section underneath, lists your recently used apps and programs. 'All apps' now shows your apps/programs listed alphabetically. The start menu also incorporates the search function directly and the Pinning process of Windows 8 makes its return for ease of access.

A couple of useful organisation features are Snap windows, now cascade out on the adjacent screen for ease of selection. Task View is also great for managing apps and programs that are open.

Windows 10's new design allows you to authenticate your identity.

For the purposes of this review, I am operating from the 10 Pro RTM build 10240. Microsoft promises to refine Windows 10 after launch, the OS moving to a more service oriented model, delivering discreet updates to features over time as they develop.

Microsoft's Stock Keeping Units (SKUs) have been provided to meet the needs of varied users in different markets and regions world-wide. To date, Windows 7 introduced the most editions of any Windows release to date (Starter, Home Basic, Home Premium, Professional, Ultimate, Enterprise, Embedded). Since the release of Windows 8, many of these editions have been consolidated to specific devices.

In addition to SKUs, Microsoft also provides specific CPU architectures tin what are known as 32 and 64 bit versions. The capability is determined specifically by how much memory your computer is able to address. The more memory, the more programs, apps and general multitasking you can complete simultaneously.

Windows 10 Home	- Cortana Assistant - Microsoft Edge web browser - Continuum tablet mode for touch-capable devices - PCs, tablets and 2-in-1s - Windows Hello face-recognition, iris and fingerprint login - universal Windows apps like Photos, Maps, Mail, Calendar, Music and Video - Ability to capture and share game play for XBOX One owners
Windows 10 Pro	- PCs, tablets and 2-in-1s - Cortana Assistant - Microsoft Edge web browser - Continuum tablet mode for touch-capable devices - Windows Hello face-recognition, iris and fingerprint login - universal Windows apps like Photos, Maps, Mail, Calendar, Music and Video - Ability to capture and share game play for XBOX One owners - Domain Join Services - BitLocker Drive Encryption - Remote Access Services - Group Policy editor - Windows Update for Business
Windows 10	- PCs, tablets and 2-in-1s

Enterprise	- Cortana Assistant - Continuum tablet mode for touch-capable devices - Windows Hello face-recognition, iris and fingerprint login - universal Windows apps like Photos, Maps, Mail, Calendar, Music and Video - Ability to capture and share game play for XBOX One owners - Domain Join Services - BitLocker Drive Encryption - Remote Access Services - Group Policy editor - Windows Update for Business - Long Term Servicing Branch - Device Guard - help protect against the ever-growing range of modern security threats targeted at devices, identities, applications and sensitive company information.
Windows 10 Education	- All the features of Windows 10 Enterprise for Academia - smaller, mobile, touch-centric devices like smartphones and small tablets - universal Windows apps
Windows 10 Mobile	- touch-optimized version of Office - Continuum for phone - productivity, security and management capabilities for customers who use their personal devices at work
Windows 10 Mobile Enterprise	- All the features of Windows 10 Mobile - Update management for businesses

The Windows 10 interface if you are coming from an older version of Windows such as Windows 7 will seem exceedingly familiar as mentioned in our overview. A big push in the early 2000's was to bring photo realistic experiences to the user interface experience such as glass and high resolution pictorial representations described using the then prevalent design trend skeumorphism. Microsoft have seemingly outgrown this stage as much of the UI has been updated with new icons and design details that are more rudimentary than needlessly edgy recognizing the universal appeal of Windows 7 even a hint of the popular Aero theme has crept back into the overarching design.

A major objective here was clearly to ease transition from the popular windows 7 design which held the bulk of users. A serious bugbear for those who braved the initial Windows 8 release was its touch optimization, putting traditional keyboard and mouse interaction on the backburner. Ultimately this produced a release that that has earned the nick name 'Vista 2'. After three years of updates, Windows 8.1 has only managed to reach 17% market share. Still substantial in comparison to Linux and the latest version of OS X, but rather underwhelming for a Windows release. Even 14-year-old Windows XP is still in active use with 12% of users still enjoying the simpler layout. Microsoft is hoping Windows 10 will right many of the wrongs of Windows 8, I personally believe it has made great waves and that the free release has been incredibly conducive to updating even the most diehard XP enthusiasts.

The most obvious change of direction is the return of the Start menu, the cornerstone of the Windows experience for nearly 20 years, Windows 10's interpretation still maintains much of its Windows 8 influences such as Modern apps, but reintroduces old favorites such as an All Apps menu, pinned apps, jump list, accessible functions such as power options and a much familiar layout. This is just the beginning of many of the changes that are step backs for the better.

The Setup Process

Upgrading to Windows 8.0 Installing from traditional DVD or USB media was a familiar experience. When it launched in 2012, the company introduced the infamous 'Upgrade Assistant' this web based installer downloaded the installation files for Windows 8.0 to your device, however this process often resulted in failure for a variety of reasons stemming from its design. The Windows 8.1 update delivered a year later was received even more poorly, a large 3.6 GB update delivered through the floundering app store. Again this update failed regularly and what is worse required a complete new download of the entire 3.6 GB each time it did so

The answer is Windows Update, which I believe should have been the first choice for Windows 8.0 and 8.1. Windows Update works like a download manager already.

It is proven and has been downloading Windows Updates and Service Packs routinely for years

Windows 10 for the first time, will be delivered to Windows 7 service pack one (The install with the greatest market share of all windows platforms) and Windows 8.1 with Update 1 just like a regular update which have both been being prepped in the run up to release with micro updates. There was also a pre check system in place users could pre-register for known as the Get Windows 10 app (GXW) this update installs the mechanisms to check your system readiness and download Windows 10 through Windows Update. Users will have seen a notification added to the system tray letting users know about the operating systems availability and the option to reserve the update and download it automatically on July 29th 2015.

This optional app had a few qualifying criteria for it to find that a user was eligible for the free upgrade:

1. Your device must be up-to-date with at least Windows 7 SP1 or Windows 8.1 Update.
2. Windows Update is turned off or is not set to receive updates automatically.
3. You've blocked or uninstalled the necessary Windows Update functionality.
4. Your device is not running genuine Windows.

5. Your Windows License is from a MSDN or TechNet subscription. If it is, you will be able to get Windows 10 through your subscription if it is still active.
6. Your computer is part of a Windows Domain
7. Microsoft has not determined your device capable of running Windows 10 even though it meets the minimum system requirements.
8. You are running a volume license client: Windows 7 Professional, Windows 7 Enterprise, Windows 8.1 Pro and Windows 8.1 Enterprise (only retail store bought or preinstalled OEM licenses) get the upgrade offer.

Download method

Users of Windows 7 and Windows 8.1 have had a new setup process in store and will have only one year to take advantage of the free upgrade offer.

Windows 10 has a piecemeal method for downloading its latest OS, allowing a background downloader which activates whenever an internet connection is established, ensuring even patchy connections can obtain the download in full. When Windows 10 is downloaded, you will be notified of the installation opportunity. You can install immediately or schedule for a more convenient time.

Happily Microsoft have dropped the necessity for an installation code as the updates all come 'pre-keyed'. So if you need to reinstall Windows 10 after one or two years from now or I install a new hard disk? Windows 10 is registered to the device, not your hard disk. Just install a new hard disk and reinstall Windows 10 and it port over through your PC's memory. With all Microsoft Account log in options still firmly in place.

An 'Out of Box' installation will prompt the user to setup a machine local account rather than the traditional Microsoft account. Microsoft has headed the various bugbears from users who felt like they were being pushed towards signing up for a Microsoft Account. This is no longer the focus based on the offline clean install I performed.

Whilst the mandatory account did have its benefits many users simply resented the holding of their information and felt that several of its features were superfluous. Microsoft Account with Windows has clear benefits, at the same time, there are a lot of users who simply don't want this functionality no matter what it offers. There does not seem to be any option to add further local accounts at present when initially logging on. Users will now create those through the Computer Management interface, control user passwords 2 or the command line.

CHAPTER 2
NEW FEATURES OVERVIEW

Windows 10 Features a significant departure from Windows 8 particularly with the integration of Microsoft's Siri competitor Cortana. We've covered many of the big changes, including Cortana integration, the return of the Start Menu and its new Gaming features.

Minor Features Overview

There have been a number of smaller upgrades which complement the raft of new larger applications well. Here I have compiled the most relevant small tips & tricks for Windows 10. Let's see whether we can't streamline your experience by learning essential keyboard shortcuts.

Keyboard shortcuts are the best way to save time when roaming Windows. Often, they're much easier to remember, than the path to a specific feature.

Windows key + A

For instance launches the new Windows 10 Action Centre. This is a novel shortcut. It's essential because not only does the Action Centre hold notifications you might have missed, you'll also find a number of handy shortcuts at the base of the screen. These pathways provide shortcuts to many of your devices external features, airplane mode, toggle tablet mode, Bluetooth and wireless connectivity as well as a shorter route to modify your display settings. The exact selection of tiles will depend on your device and can be added to if needed.

Using Windows Key + I

Launches Windows 10's Settings App. This was an innovation designed to phase out rummaging through the control panel for every minor change and seems very well put together as time saving applications go. Unfortunately some advanced features are missing but can still be accessed through the remains of the Control Panel, either by searching in the Settings app or by clicking the Windows key and performing a search.

Windows Key + X

Launches the 'Power User Menu'. New to Windows 10 the menu features direct command prompt access with options for administrator access straight away without additional button clicks. The shortcut itself has been around for a while. In Windows 7, it opened the Windows Mobility Centre. Since Windows 8 this shortcut has launched the power user menu, which contains access to all advanced Windows features including the Mobility Centre, Computer Management, Control Panel, Command Prompt elevated, and shut down options. It's not new but has slipped out in the comparative lull of Windows 8's in-illustrious reign so it has been included here as it's good to know how to access the basic functions. To learn what else you can do with your keyboard in Windows, consult our Windows Shortcuts 101 guide.

Extend Battery Life with Battery Saver

Does exactly what it says on the tin by limiting the amount of background applications running, controlling display settings etc, relatively small steps but every little helps. This innovation can be launched by a quick press of Windows + I to launch the Settings app, selecting System > Battery saver > Battery saver settings, check the box to enable the feature, and pick a percentage at which you want it to do its job.

For the particularly sceptical you can see just how much this process is saving you by taking the following steps to review wastage via background processes Under System > Battery saver > Battery usage If this number is large, you might want to examine what's starting up with Windows and take steps such as enable Battery Saver at a higher percentage or review your permissions

Time saving options

The release of Windows 8 bought Microsoft's dedicated team a new challenge which was to reengineer the Windows boot up experience. One of their strategies to make the total boot up time appear faster was to delay the launch of applications. This feature known as start-up delay has survived the transition in to Windows 10. If you run Windows 10 on a particularly high spec machine and have experienced very fast boot times, but are stuck with apps which will not be available immediately, you might benefit from disabling this start up delay which largely functions by streamlining this boot up.

CHAPTER 3
PROS AND CONS OF UPGRADING TO WINDOWS 10

Main Improvements

1. Refreshed icons and graphical choices.
2. The upgrade is free for Windows 7 and Windows 8.1 users
3. minimal learning curve, familiar user experience
4. The infamous Media Centre has been axed entirely, I'm throwing this in the Pro's sections as I personally enjoy the replacement however if you *need* media center there is no support at all for it in windows 10 which could be a deal breaker as it will automatically uninstall this software meaning the best option if you wish to keep media center would be to run it on an older platform.
5. Microsoft have stated that 'they will provide a DVD playback
6. Cortana Integration with Microsoft's digital assistant – Cortana users can now use this for finding and retrieving information on the Internet as well as locally stored information, such as files or programs. The program is now capable of controlling applications such as the Music Player or prepare an email message or track a parcel.
7. Task View has been altered for managing applications using multiple desktops.
8. Modern apps can now be integrated in the snap style windowing system and behave the same way as desktop apps.
9. Notification Center for centralized management of notifications and quick access to PC settings.

10. Universal applications are now able to function cross platform on a multitude of devices.
11. Windows 10 PC, but also your mobile phone running Windows 10 and also XBOX One.
12. Productive App centered environment for users to add
13. Windows Hello and Passport for personalized authentication without the use of passwords.
14. Improved setup and recovery tools (rollback), backup
15. BOX App for Streaming of live games to a PC or Tablet
16. Office applications Word, Excel, Outlook, OneNote and PowerPoint have been further touch optimized. This means that Office can be used on all devices with touch support. Users can edit, prepare documents, spreadsheets and presentations with full document fidelity regardless of which platform they run windows on.
17. Continuum Mode - if you own a 2 in 1 device that works both as a laptop and tablet, you can easily let Windows 10 decide the best settings for you. Once detached into Tablet mode for instance, you can work in a more touch optimized user interface. Users will also be able to remotely use Windows 10 Mobile apps on their Windows PCs.
18. Support for media formats such as FLAC and MKV
19. Microsoft Edge has replaced the notoriously slow internet explorer for Windows 10 and support advances in Windows 10 such as Cortana for finding information on the web, Annotation, PDF support, superior reading experience.
20. Music and playlist integration in OneDrive.
21. Unified messaging using Skype Integration.

22. Device Guard is another minor upgrade for protecting devices against malicious applications.

Which features will be removed when I upgrade from a previous version of Windows?

What is being lost?

- Watching DVDs requires separate playback software as media center is gone.
- Windows 7 desktop gadgets will be removed as part of installing Windows 10.
- Windows 10 Home users will have updates from Windows Update automatically available. Windows 10 Pro and Windows 10 Enterprise users will have the ability to defer updates.
- Users currently running Windows 7 Home Premium, Windows 7 Professional, Windows 7 Ultimate, Windows 8 Pro with Media Center, or Windows 8.1 Pro with Media Center and you install Windows 10, Windows Media Center will be removed completely.
- Solitaire, Minesweeper, and Hearts Games that come pre-installed on Windows 7 have now been removed as part of the transition to Windows 10. Microsoft has separately released a version of Solitaire and Minesweeper called the "Microsoft Solitaire Collection" and "Microsoft Minesweeper."
- If you are still sporting a USB floppy disk drive, you will need to download the new drivers from Windows Update or possibly the manufacturer's website.

- If you have Windows Live Essentials installed on your system, the OneDrive application is removed and replaced with the inbox version of OneDrive.
- No Media Centre will be available at all Persons who need to use Media Center should consider carefully before upgrading from their previous version of Windows. The Windows 10 upgrade will automatically remove any installations of Media Center.
- Windows Virtual PC with Windows XP Mode will no longer work for the foreseeable future until updated by the developers.

CHAPTER 4
MANAGING & ORGANIZING DESKTOP SPACE

Virtual desktops were finally added as a built-in feature in Windows 10. If you've used a Mac or Linux, you'd know that this can be a very useful feature. If you are a multi tasker and open several programs up at once, this feature allows you to keep them organized.

Using Virtual Desktops in Windows 10

The virtual desktops feature in Windows 10 is called "Task View" and is located on the Taskbar.

Clicking on the "Task View" button brings up the Task View interface, where you can see your open windows on virtual desktops you've added. When you open the Task View interface for the first time, or you only have one desktop, the "Add a desktop" button is available. Click it to add another virtual desktop.

Now, when you click the "Task View" button, all of your desktops will be displayed on the Task View interface. In the example below, there are no windows open on either of the desktops.

If you have program windows open on your desktops, they show the thumbnails of the desktops on the Task View interface. When you move your mouse over a desktop on the Task View interface, the open programs on that desktop display as large thumbnails above the Task View interface. Click on one of the large thumbnails to make that program (and the desktop) active. It's similar to the old Alt + Tab feature from previous versions of Windows. Click on a desktop on the Task View interface to make that desktop active.

You can switch desktops using the keyboard, as well. To do this, press the Windows key + Tab. The programs on the currently active desktop display as large thumbnails, as discussed above and the thumbnail for the currently active program on that desktop is outlined. Now, press Tab again. This removes the outline from the active program thumbnail and Task View interface active. Use the arrow keys to move among the desktops on the Task View interface. When you have highlighted the desktop to which you want to switch, press Enter.

Windows indicates when a program is open on other desktop be putting a line under that program's icon on the Taskbar. Clicking the icon not only activates the program, but also the desktop on which it is open.

You can move programs among the different desktops you've set up. To do so, switch to the desktop containing the program you want to move. Click the "Task View" button on the Taskbar. Right-click on the large thumbnail for the program you want to move, select "Move to," and then select the desktop number to which you want to move the program.

The program now displays on the other desktop

To close a desktop, click the "Task View" button on the Taskbar to bring up the Task View interface. Move your mouse over the thumbnail for the desktop you want to close. Click the X button that displays in the upper-right corner of the thumbnail.

NOTE: If you close a desktop that has open programs on it, those programs are then transferred to the next desktop to the left of the one you're closing.

If you're using a touch screen computer or device, you can access the Task View or virtual desktops, by swiping in from the left. This feature replaces the old application switcher for both touch and non-touch screen devices.

-

The newest Desktop Optimization Pack (MDOP) was released and it also supports Windows 10. MDOP contains virtualization tools to manage, deploy and monitor key Windows applications and features along with its system recovery potential. Here's the latest on MDOP.

MDOP 2015, which is available to Microsoft Developer Network (MSDN) subscribers, contains Microsoft Advanced Group Policy Management, Microsoft User Experience Virtualization, Microsoft Application Virtualization for Windows Desktops, the Microsoft Diagnostics and Recovery Toolset, Microsoft BitLocker, Microsoft Enterprise Desktop Virtualization and Administration and Monitoring.

Here's what's new in the new pack:

For App-V 5.1 (Microsoft Application Virtualization)

- Support for Windows 10
- Import and export the manifest file
- Improved look and feel to the Management Console
- Import and export virtual registry keys
- Import a directory into the virtual file system
- Improved functionality in the Sequencer
- Support in Package Converter for multiple scripts on a single event trigger
- Enable or disable Browser Helper Objects

For MBAM 2.5 SP1 (Microsoft BitLocker Administration and Monitoring)

- Ability to automatically unlock the TPM after a lockout

- Support for Microsoft SQL Server 2014 SP1
- Ability to escrow OwnerAuth passwords without owning the TPM
- System Center 2012 R2 Configuration Manager SP2 and Support for Windows 10
- Functionality that enables BitLocker using MBAM as part of a Windows deployment
- MBAM Client now supports 13 new languages
- Support for FIPS-compliant BitLocker numerical password protectors

UEV 2.1 SP1 (Microsoft User Experience Virtualization)

- Support for Windows 10
- Compatibility with Microsoft Azure
- Support Added for Roaming Network Printers

DaRT 10 (Microsoft Diagnostics and Recovery

- Support for Windows 10
- AGPM 4.0 SP3
- Removal of Windows Defender from DaRT tools
- Support for Windows 10
- Improved process for upgrading

Why Should I use Windows 10 Manager?

- Windows 10 is the newest Operating System for home users and professionals alike. Windows 10 brings clarity to your world, so you can more safely and easily accomplish everyday tasks and instantly find what you want on your PC.

-

Windows 10 Manager is the superior software tool that allows you to optimize and tweak your software, it bundles more than 40 different utilities into one and help your system faster and more stable, secure and personal!

-

-

Features and Benefits of Windows 10 Manager

-

Get detailed system and all hardware information on your system; help you find out the installation key of Windows, Office products; show all detailed information of running processes and threads on your machine; Windows 10 Manager offers 1-clicking Cleaner cleans your system automatically; Repair Centre helps you to fix various system   problems.

-

  ▶   Optimizer:

- Tweak your system to improve windows start-up and shutdown speed, tweak your hardware to increase system speed and performance; Control what is started on Windows start-up, check and repair the advanced start-up items to restore the malicious change by viruses; Tune up and optimize system services and Task Schedule, turn off smartly some unnecessary system services and tasks to improve   system   performance.

-
- ▸ Cleaner:

- Find out which folders or files take up the most room in your disk space and can be viewed with; Smart Uninstaller which can completely delete programs from your system without Registry entries and residual files; Duplicate Files Finder can scan your computer for files with the same size, name and modification time; Clean junk files to increase Hard Disk space; Registry Cleaner repairs and checks improperly linked Registry entries. Desktop Cleaner can clean useless icons and files on the Desktop easily. Registry Defrag re-indexes and rebuilds your registry to reduce its access time and improve responsiveness at the same time.
-
-

- ▸ Customization:

- Customize the look of your system by tweaking system Explorer, Desktop, Start Menu, Taskbar and notification area; Manage the pinned items and can pin any files or folders to Taskbar and Start Screen; Create the quick start-up items on Taskbar with the Jump List launcher. Tune up

Windows 10 boot menu; Edit context menus of mouse Right-Clicking; Edit easily the Win + X menu that shown when right-click on Desktop bottom-left corner or Win + X keyboard shortcut ; Create the shortcut that executed quick on run dialog box. Visual Customizer can change system and file type icons, change the lock screen image automatically.

-
-

  ▶ Security:

- Enhance system security by adjusting system components, login and UAC settings. Tune up System Restore options; Restrict and hide to access programs and drives; Decrypt/encrypt files and move system folders to safe or memorable locations; Restore the files that accidentally formatted or deleted on disk; Privacy Protector enables you to maintain your personal privacy by wiping the tracks that you leave behind; Hide, add or delete the Control Panel entries.

-
-

  ▶ Network:

- Optimize your Internet connection speed, manage all shares items; Tweak the Microsoft Edge and Internet Explorer easily; IP Switcher can switch your IP address easily on different networks; Edits the Hosts file to speed up surfing internet and permit only to access the specified Hosts.

-
-

  ▶ Misc. Utilities:

-

  Show the collection of Windows utilities and pin system items to Start Screen and Taskbar; split and merge any files; automatically backs up files regularly using Super Copy. Registry Tools help you to operate Registry easily.

CHAPTER 5
PERSONALISING WINDOWS 10

With Windows 10 comes making it personal. Getting the look of the operating system ↗ you'll be spending so much time looking at just right, pleasing to your eyes.

Besides just wallpaper and a theme color, Microsoft is including new settings to let users enable or disable transparency across the Start menu, taskbar, and Action Centre. You'll also notice a new animation effect on elements inside of each of the setting's sections. Here's how to make Windows 10 your own.

How to access Personalization

Finding your way to Personalization is straightforward, just launch the Settings apps, and click Personalization. If you find yourself accessing these settings quite often, you can click the Pin icon in the top-right corner to pin a tile to the Start menu for quicker access.

Personalizing the Windows 10 desktop

The Personalization settings page contains four new sections: Background, Colors, Lock screen and Themes.

Background

The Background section is self-explanatory. This area is the place where you can set a new desktop wallpaper, a solid color, or a slide show.

Colors

The Colors section is where all the interesting changes are happening. In Colors, you can adjust a variety of settings. Here you will find the 'automatically pick a color from my background' option. When this is enabled, the feature will analyse the background image extracting the primary color and setting it on the Start menu, taskbar, and Action Centre.

The technical preview phase introduced a new dark theme in the Start menu, taskbar, and Action Centre. This theme will be the default theme when the Show color on taskbar and Start menu is disabled. Sliding the switch to the On position will enable scheme color to flow from a custom color selection or the primary color coming from your current background.

Finally, Microsoft is adding the Make Start menu transparent option, which not only will enable or disable the transparency for the Start menu, but also controls the transparency for the taskbar and Action Center.

Furthermore, if you need to change the high contrast color settings, Microsoft has added a convenient link right into Colors as well.

Lock screen

In the Lock screen, under the Background settings, you can configure to show a picture or a slide show. You can also choose the "Windows spotlight" option, which apparently is a new feature that pulls random background from the internet.

From the Lock screen section, you can choose which apps show notifications, but this is nothing new.

Themes

Microsoft is also moving the Theme's settings to the Settings app.

Wrapping things up

While there many changes new options to personalize Windows 10, there is still a lot of room for improvement.

Currently, there is no way for users to customize the level of the transparency like on Xbox One, for example.

CHAPTER 6
TRACKING SYSTEM

Tracking Protection helps you stay in control of your privacy as you browse the web.

Some of the content, images, ads, and analytics that you see on the websites you visit are provided by outside or third-party websites. While this content can provide value to both your favorite websites and you, these third-party websites have the ability to potentially track your behavior across multiple sites. Tracking Protection provides you an added level of control and choice about the information that third-party websites can potentially use to track your browsing activity.

With Tracking Protection Lists, you can choose which third-party sites can receive your information and track you online. By adding a list, you can block content from websites that might have an impact on your privacy. When you add a Tracking Protection List, Internet Explorer will prevent your information from being sent by limiting data requests to websites in the list. For each list that you add, the setting applies across all pages and websites you visit, not just the pages you get the lists from. And each time you hegin a new browsing session, the blocking stays on until you decide to turn it off.

Get Tracking Protection Lists

Windows 10 hasn't quite made it a week out of the gate without causing an uproar of controversy.

It's not a big surprise. For months ahead of the operating system's launch, news has trickled out that the software is tracking your location, collecting data on you, and uploads your Wi-Fi passwords to your friends.

From both sides of the fence: Some have said Microsoft does not respect its users' privacy by default; others believe some of the hype is overblown. Perhaps the biggest critique is that upon setup, the process could offer more granular options, and report less data back to the software giant.

All of the tracking mechanisms can be switched off through the various options at setup, and after the fact through the settings.

But now there's a lightweight, open-source app that aims to claw back your privacy.

"In my opinion, there's some unnecessary fear concerning Windows 10, but beneath all of that I do believe lots of the fear is justified," said Syed Qazi, the app's developer, on his motives about the app.

Among the options, there's an app called "Disable Windows 10 Tracking" which disables certain Windows services, disables telemetry collection and other tracking. The code is also available on GitHub for inspection.

CHAPTER 7
WINDOWS 10 TOP TRICKS & TIPS

Since the new release of Windows 10 and much of the loyal customer base have already got it up and running, I'll be discussing some of the best hidden tips, features and tricks in the functioning system. If you're still on the fence, take note: You really do want Windows 10, despite a lot of the gripes we've shared over the past several months. It's worth getting on the list for (or <u>downloading the Windows 10 ISO directly</u>). It combines the best of Windows 8 — super-fast start-up, improved security — with much of what made Windows 7 familiar and easy to use and without trying to force you to buy a touch screen or learn a whole set of hidden UI gestures.

If you're a computer nut like me, tweaking the OS is always the fun part. Discovering and implementing power user tips are my favorite part of getting a major new version of an OS. I still remember back when DOS 5.0 came out, and I was running DOS 3.3, and I got to try all these new things to optimize my 286. (We've come a long way.) Nostalgia aside, here's what you need to know to amp up your <u>Windows 10</u> install and take it to the next level.

Task view and virtual desktops

An awesome attribute that the Windows 10 has is how it copes with virtual desktops. The fact that it can even handle them at all, is a great improvement to the system, since Linux and Mac OS X users have had that opportunity for a much longer time. It lets you set up a series of tasks and windows on your desktop↗, your email and Twitter window on another, and a third for general Web browsing and research. To get started, click the Task View icon on the taskbar (immediately to the right of the Search box), or hold down the Windows key (abbreviated throughout as Win) and Tab.

Configure privacy settings

When you're first setting up Windows 10, make sure to select a Custom install so you can modify the privacy settings, instead of going with the Express install. (If you already installed it, no worries; you can fix it all in Settings). Otherwise you'll find yourself agreeing to all sorts of private data sharing↗ — and while Windows 10 is free for Windows 7 and Windows 8 users, it's not a free product in and of itself — so there's no reason to share your personal information when it's not required.

Print to PDF

You can finally print a document (or rather, save it) as PDF without using a third-party utility. This makes it much easier to save and distribute documents that aren't easily modified. Another long overdue feature makes it in under the radar.

Make sure Wi-Fi Sense is off

You may feel differently about this, but I certainly don't like the idea of allowing access to my Wifi network unless I specifically give out the password. Here's <u>how to make sure your computer isn't doing that</u> — and if it is, how to turn it off.

Run it in a virtual machine

If you're thinking of taking the Windows 10 plunge, but don't want to disturb your machine that's currently running just fine, here's <u>how to install Windows 10 in a virtual machine</u> first. Note that this is different than the virtual desktops. I mentioned above; it's virtualizing the entire OS within another OS (your existing one).

Windows Explorer Home tab and Quick Access

Windows Explorer windows are a lot more useful this time around, thanks to a new Home tab (pictured above). It makes file copies a cinch. If you look at the top left of the window, you'll see a new Quick Access group that lets you navigate to recently accessed folders. That makes it much easier to maintain a fast workflow as you navigate around your computer's file system.

Customize the Start Menu

The new Start Menu is such a huge improvement over what came with Windows 8.1 that it's almost impossible to describe the relief. It combines the best elements of Windows 7 and Windows 8. And it's also fully customizable. I admit the first thing I did is unpin all of Microsoft's tiles and then shrink the size of the menu so it looks a lot like Windows 7 (pictured).

For a while, during some of the Windows 10 Technical Preview builds, you could pin the Recycle Bin to the taskbar, which makes it a bit more like OS X. Unfortunately that functionality seems to be gone in the release version, although you can still attach it to the Start Menu.

Command prompt tweaks

Many of the Windows 10 utilities still look as they did in Windows 7 and 8. But one of the unseen changes is in the Command Prompt — head over to Properties and you'll suddenly find you can enable a host of customizations, including a transparent background, resizing the window and word wrap.

Battery saver

If you're on a laptop and your battery is running low, Windows 10 is smart enough to begin throttling back background services and other threads so that you can squeeze the last bit of battery life out of your machine. To enable Battery Saver, click the Start menu and head to Settings | System | Battery Saver.

Background scrolling

Ever notice how when you hover your mouse cursor over a

window and try and scroll, you still can't, because the window wasn't active? Turn this feature on in Settings | Devices | Mouse and Touchpad and you'll be able to do just that.

Keyboard shortcuts

Here are some keyboard shortcuts you may want to be aware of — ones that will help your daily workflow:

- Windows Key-Tab (Task View)
- Windows Key-Ctrl-D (new virtual desktop)
- Windows Key-Right-Up (Moves app to top right quadrant)
- Windows Key-Ctrl-Left or Right (virtual desktop)
- Windows Key-Up and Down (snap apps to top or bottom of screen or maximizes)
- Windows Key-Ctrl-C (Cortana listening)
- Windows Key-Ctrl-F4 (closes virtual desktop)
- Windows Key-S (Daily Glance for weather, news, sports)

OneDrive integration

Free cloud storage is a godsend these days, and Microsoft makes it super easy in Windows 10 with OneDrive. You can use it to store files for mobile device access from iOS or Android and you can even set it to let you access any file on your PC remotely — not just the ones you drag over to your OneDrive folder.

Xbox Streaming

Windows 10 has finally added an Xbox integration and you can use it to log into your Xbox Live account. But more importantly, you can use it to stream Xbox One games locally on your PC. You'll have to enable it first on the Xbox One under Settings | Preferences | Allow game streaming, and then on the PC in the Xbox application. (Interestingly, Microsoft is also going the other way and adding keyboard and mouse support to the Xbox One — not that you'll need that, since you've already got a PC.)

Find the original Control Panel (and other goodies)

The new Settings panel is easy to navigate and makes more sense than the crafty old Control Panel, but you'll still need the latter to access some deeper options in the system. It's easy to call up, even though it's hidden; just right click on the Start button on the bottom left of the screen and choose it from the pop-up menu, or type Control Panel in the Search bar at the bottom left in the taskbar. When you right-click the Start button, you'll see all kinds of useful things there, such as Computer Management and Disk Management; for what it's worth, those options bring you right back to the familiar Windows 7-style apps in each case.

CONCLUSION

The end of an era! That is how it honestly felt when I started this journey writing about Windows 10. It's no surprise, the 90s and even the 2000s have been filled with reviews of technologies such as operating systems that are written in thousands of words; I personally looked forward to reading them, but looking at the future, this methodology of covering the latest version of a Windows release will eventually come to an end. Windows 10 is certainly the last major (what they call big bang) release of the company's popular desktop operating system. I have been evaluating Windows 10 since October 1st 2014 and I have managed to the see the operating system go through its ups and downs during that time. The experience has afforded me the ability to have an intimate experience with this platform.

A lot has changed since 2006 when Windows Vista came to market, a colossus overhaul of a platform that almost brought down the entire industry with it and at the same time giving rise to old and new players. The Internet certainly facilitated the changing landscape of how we use and consume technology. The 80's and 90's encouraged the upgrade treadmill which encouraged users and companies to take advantage of the latest advances in computing when they became available, processors, memory, graphics, software. In a sense, we are almost going back to those days but in a way that does not present the disruptive painstaking migration that was always a certainty when migrating to newer operating system revisions every 3 to 5 years. Microsoft missed the number 9 and went with 10, because they believe that it is a perfect 10.but once you start installing it should only take about 20-45 minutes to install windows 10, it does feature some minor modifications to previous versions, and you are greeted with a Welcome Back screen which allows you to sign in and complete setup.

Windows 10 presents a challenge in a market that has pretty much migrated to the Internet. It's at a cross road between a world that is old and new. Since Windows 8 came to market in late 2012, it has been met with mixed reviews. The bold strategy behind that release left behind a market of more than a billion users who have enjoyed working on desktop and laptop computers using mouse/touchpad and keyboard for more than two decades. The consistent evolution of the Windows interface since Windows 95 gave users the confidence about how they operated a PC. Using a Windows PC for most users came naturally because of the platforms ubiquity and interface standards. Microsoft promises to continue refining Windows 10 even after it launches the OS moving to a more service focused model, delivering smaller pockets of features over time when they are ready. Throughout the many revisions of Windows, Microsoft has provided a variety of editions or what are known as Stock Keeping Units (SKUs) to meet the vastly developing needs of users. To date, Windows 7 introduced the most editions (Starter, Home Basic, Home Premium, Professional, Ultimate, Enterprise and Embedded).

Windows 8 took most of its influence from its mobile sibling Windows Phone OS which was practically unknown and lacked the market penetration to provide a familiar transplant to the desktop. A mixture of bad execution, lack of modern applications and questionable design decisions made Windows 8, the company's Vista 2. This even resulted in the company having to scramble to tone down a lot of the earlier design choices a year later with a revision called Windows 8.1 and another major update seven months later called Update 1.

Should I upgrade?

The first thing you'll probably be thinking about, is there benefits? Software over the years, no matter if it is Linux, Windows or OS X have matured incredibly. The fact that Windows XP (2001), a version of Windows four generations behind is still in heavy use is a testament to how much the platform that is 'Windows' has reached a very good enough point in computing lives of many persons. 2009's Windows 7 is the most popular release to date, running on 1 billion systems worldwide. Even when Windows 10 launches, both Windows 7 and Windows 8.1 will continue to be supported at the end of the decade and many users will keep running them for a variety of reasons, personal preference, look and feel, Media Center, stick it to the man.

You can customize the look of your system by tweaking system Explorer, Desktop, Start Menu, Taskbar and notification area; Manage the pinned items and can pin any files or folders to Taskbar and Start Screen; Create the quick start up items on Taskbar with the Jump List launcher; Tune up Windows 10 boot menu; Edit context menus of mouse Right-Clicking; Edit easily the Win + X menu that shown when right-click on Desktop bottom-left corner or Win + X keyboard shortcut ; Create the shortcut that executed quick on run dialog box. Visual Customizer can change system and file type icons, change the lock screen image automatically.

One of the best things about Windows 10 is how it handles virtual desktops. The fact that it finally handles them at all, out of the box, is a great step, since Mac OS X and Linux users have had that capability for a long time. It lets you set up a series of tasks and windows on your desktop, your email and Twitter window on another, and a third for general Web browsing and research.

I have already made my decision; yes, I will upgrade all my computers to Windows 10. I am able to make this decision because of a number of factors. For the average user who probably just started learning about Windows 10 a couple months ago, a few days ago or even a few months from now, this will be a critical decision to make. Microsoft has righted many wrongs with this release. Thoughtfully refining three years of chaos to produce a product that many users will like. Customizable Start menu, Action

Center, Snap Assist, robust modern applications blended with a bit touch and blossomed into a perfect balance and delightful experience that is desktop productivity at its best.

With the continued rapid growth of competing platforms such as Android and iOS, both of which own nearly 100 percent of the mobile market have left Microsoft in a position of defending its legacy. A strong legacy and I believe Microsoft has produced release of Windows that restarts the platform on a foundation of innovation for years to come. Striking the right balance is what has made Windows 10 the best client operating system out of any (iOS, Android and Linux).

Bold statements I know and at the end of the day, your operating system is only as good as the apps that are available for it. Microsoft has refocused itself over the past couple of years setting a direction as the company that defines productivity. Windows 10 is the epitome of that vision, it works across a wealth of form factors and services, delivering experiences that maximizes a user's investment in technology that suits them. Whether it's a Windows 10 Mobile device with Continuum, a Surface Hub in a meeting, a Tablet used by a student, a designer mocking up layouts in Photoshop or a home user composing a simple email message, Windows 10 has achieved a powerful vision of one.

DID YOU ENJOY THIS BOOK?

I want to thank you for purchasing and reading this book. I really hope you got a lot out of it.

Can I ask a quick favor though?

If you enjoyed this book I would really appreciate it if you could leave me a positive review on Amazon.

I love getting feedback from my customers and reviews on Amazon really do make a difference. I read all my reviews and would really appreciate your thoughts.

Thanks so much.

Bill Vickers

www.ingramcontent.com/pod-product-compliance
Lightning Source LLC
Chambersburg PA
CBHW061101050326
40690CB00034B/1953